Congratulations!
You're Going To Be A
Grandmother

Congratulations! You're Going To Be A Grandmother

LANIE CARTER

Illustrations by
Elli Carter Stacey

OAK TREE PUBLICATIONS, INC.
PUBLISHERS
LA JOLLA, CALIFORNIA

DEDICATED WITH LOVE
TO MY GRANDCHILDREN,
DAYNA, BRYAN, BROOKE AND ARON,
AND TO THE
MANY OTHER BABIES
WHO HAVE TOUCHED
MY LIFE.

First Edition.
Manufactured in the United States of America.
For information write to: Oak Tree Publications,
P.O. Box 1012, La Jolla, CA 92038

Library of Congress Cataloging in Publication Data

Carter, Lanie.
  Congratulations, you're going to be a grandmother.

  1. Grandparents—United States. I. Title.
HQ759.9.C37   306.8'7   80-13415

ISBN 0-916392-48-1

CONTENTS

INTRODUCTION *1*

NEW NAME, NEW ROLE *11*

THE MORE THINGS CHANGE, THE MORE
THEY STAY THE SAME *29*

THE NEW FAMILY *39*

THE BEST IS YET TO COME *63*

1457

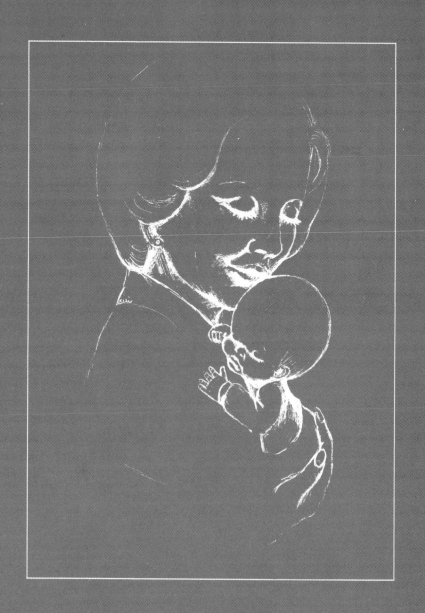

INTRODUCTION

Grandmothering is a gentle art, and Lanie Carter may be its most skilled practitioner. The publication of this book is a natural development in the life of a remarkable woman whose career is loving babies and their parents.

Lanie Carter is a New Yorker transplanted to California. She married young, before finishing college, and immersed herself in the traditional role of wife and homemaker. She loved her job. Her four children were born during the New York years, and Lanie was able to observe her own mother as a "terrific" Auntie Mame-type grandmother—a sophisticated, loving lady who took one child at a time on trips to the city for mysterious delights. Abruptly, Bill Carter was lured away to Southern California and the family then experienced the isolation from grandparents and loving "others," which Lanie would later recognize as a common affliction of young, mobile families.

In general, though, the family prospered in its new setting and, as the last child entered school, Lanie devoted herself to various projects. In the early sixties, she became a "Pink Lady" at our new community hospital and (with the immense charm which has always melted opposition) became the first volunteer on the post-partum floor—the new-mothers' area which had long been off-limits to outsiders. Her duties led her frequently past the nursery where one day she asked about a baby girl who had been languishing there for some weeks. On learning that the child was awaiting a foster home, Lanie asked to take her. Her response to being refused, characteristically, was to go home and apply for her own foster-home license. Eight months later, Lanie was the temporary, but enormously affectionate, mother of a ten-pound red-head named Peter. Peter was followed by a steady succession of infants of all types and temperaments who were loved and cuddled and soothed in the Carter household.

Then Bill Carter became ill and it was impossible to take more babies. However, as her husband seemed to improve, Lanie began working part-time in the office of a local pediatrician, as a receptionist. There, in a casual way, she began sharing her accumulated wisdom about infants with the mothers in the waiting room. Eventually the doctor began asking her to help an occasional family with an infant who was failing to thrive. Lanie would take the child home for a time, and soon the baby would relax and grow—and so would the parents. In her non-judgmental, easy way, Lanie was now teaching parenting, as well as perfecting the art of handling even the most "difficult" infants.

Up to this point, Lanie's activities were a pleasant avocation, but after her husband died in 1972 she began thinking about a full-time career, partly (as she says now) to conquer an overwhelming feeling that her own life was over. She joined our pediatric office staff in 1973, again as a receptionist, although she soon asked permission to provide non-medical advice about infant care. As her competence clearly matched her enthusiasm, we were happy to have her help the new mothers. Lanie spent another year finding out everything new parents wanted to know about babies, and then presented us with an original proposal: she would provide regular prenatal classes in our office, daily visits in the hospital to the new mothers (in addition to the doctor's visits), and a 24-hour telephone service for parents needing answers to simple, urgent non-medical questions. This was at a time when most of our expectant parents were already attending classes in preparation for childbirth; but no one at that time was talking much about the newborn himself, and less about such predictable parental emotions as nervousness, fatigue and "the blues." Lanie was not interested in being another paramedical practitioner. She viewed her role as that of a caring, sympathetic and unusually well-informed and objective grandmother.

In that role, Lanie's success has been phenomenal. Her pioneering work for our office was instantly appreciated, and it was soon apparent that no other service we provided was more valued by our patients. The local newspaper, and eventually the international press, published reports about "the world's first professional grandmother," and the letters of praise and inquiry began to come in from all over the country. It was clear that Lanie's work responded to a widespread need that was not being met in other ways.

Finally the inevitable happened; it became obvious that Lanie's services should be offered to the whole community and not just to families served by a single office. A unique position of "New Family Care Coordinator" was created for her by the community hospital, and there Lanie continues all her previous activities with the families of every infant born at the hospital. In addition, she conducts a class called "Adjusting to Parenthood" for families with six-week and six-month-old babies, and—not surprisingly—takes numerous telephone calls about her vast brood of older "grandchildren," many of whom are now in school.

In her "spare" time she has written a warm and wise book called *Congratulations! You're Going to Be a Grandmother.*

Sarita Doyle Eastman, M.D.

Dear Grandma,

I came to write this book because . . . Well, because I'm the kind of woman who must always
have a baby in her arms. Even when I was a child,
I could never resist peeking into passing baby
carriages.

When I grew up and married, I had my own
babies, and I had a husband who was just as child-
centered as I was. While we were rearing our own
four children, we were also foster parents, and we
burped, diapered, patted and fed babies who
needed extra attention while their families were
going through difficult times.

After Bill passed away and my children left for
college, or married and moved into homes of their
own, there was a great void in my life. I had an
empty house, with no husband and no babies, and
when a neighborhood physician offered me a job, I
jumped at the chance to get out of that empty

house and into a busy pediatric office full of squalling infants, worried mothers and ringing telephones.

Often, when I answered the telephone, I found myself talking to an anxious new mother. Sometimes she only wanted a simple answer to a non-medical problem. "What should I buy for the layette?" said one girl. Another wanted to know if it was okay to use a regular laundry detergent on her baby's things. Some callers just needed reassurance that their babies were doing fine. Young mothers do not automatically know that it's all right for a baby to cry, or that hiccups don't signal the beginning of a horrid disease. They may also need to be told that a newborn can sneeze even if he doesn't have a cold.

Soon, with the blessings of my three "baby doctors," I was giving non-medical advice to the new mothers. It was the kind of advice a grandmother might give and I saw that it filled a need. In our modern, transient world, many young mothers are separated by thousands of miles from their own moms and they can't easily benefit from the child-rearing experience of a grandmother's generation.

I researched what new parents needed to know about babies and in 1974 I started having classes for expectant parents in the doctor's office. I also started making daily visits to the hospital to talk to the new young parents, and my doctors arranged for a twenty-four hour answering service so that the young mothers and the fathers could call me whenever problems arose.

Without quite meaning to do it, I had become perhaps the world's first professional grandmother, and in 1978 Scripps Hospital in San Diego gave me a salary and a classroom so that I could teach prenatal classes and could make daily visits to the new families and talk with mothers, fathers and grandparents.

Frequently I met grandmothers who had come to help with the baby. They were almost always bright-eyed with anticipation, but too often I learned later on that the grandmother left days ahead of schedule because of "friction in the household."

The more I heard this, the more it bothered me. I began to ask the new parents and the new grandmothers what went wrong. As I listened to the answers, I became convinced that, with some planning, these unhappy situations could and should be avoided.

More and more children today grow up in families where both parents work. Some children are being raised in single-parent families. In such a time, a child needs to learn about his roots, and the grandparents are the roots. If today's nuclear family can become, to a degree, the extended family comprised of three generations, with all the caring and strength that results from such a unit, our grandchildren can be happier and more secure as they grow up.

I have never been a grandfather, so I don't presume to speak to grandfathers. I know about grandmothers, however, and I know that the bond between Grandmother and the new mother—and the new grandchild—is like no other.

So this book is dedicated to Grandma—a lucky person, and a very special one.

Lanie Carter

NEW NAME, NEW ROLE

Barbara is probably a typical grandmother. She heard about her daughter's pregnancy when her daughter telephoned after her visit to the doctor. Her daughter was happy and a little bit frightened. Barbara was happy and, as she later confessed, just a tiny bit dismayed. "You can't kid yourself that you're still young when you're a grandmother," she told me. "When you're a grandmother, you're beginning to get up there."

Even before she told her husband, Barbara called several of her close friends and invited them for coffee. When they arrived, she found herself becoming flushed and excited. She found herself beginning to make plans and she wondered aloud whether she should give a shower for her daughter.

"You don't give the shower when you're the grandmother," said one of her friends. "All you have to do is go to it."

"Oh," said Barbara, and she wondered whether she should be pleased or disappointed. She decided almost immediately that she was pleased. Giving showers was one thing that Barbara truly had never cared for.

In the weeks that followed, Barbara learned more about the things she wouldn't have to do: She would not have to paint a room for the new baby, or even decide what color the room would be painted. She would not have to stay on a diet or have backaches or throw up in the mornings. She would not have to do breathing exercises, and eventually she would not have to go into a hospital and have the baby.

"I thought at first it was going to be a lot of work," said Barbara. "I don't know why I thought that, except maybe that new little people up till then had been a lot of work. It took me a while to catch on, but I did finally figure out that being a grandmother is the fun part! I get to do what I really enjoy, and the part that's a drudge I leave alone."

Barbara went shopping for her grandchild and bought pink things, since she hoped the new baby would be a girl. She also bought a plush doggie which played a tune when it was wound with a key and which was much more expensive than anything she had ever bought for her own children.

The baby was born and it was a boy, but Barbara did not even worry about the pink things she had bought. She went right out and got some in blue. She told me that the baby looked a lot like her husband, and that he had big feet and would probably be tall like his Uncle Jack.

"Only I think he'll be better looking than Jack," said Barbara. "They're like little miracles, aren't they? Every time one is born, we're getting another chance to go back and do it over—and do it right!"

Barbara's sense of fulfillment upon the birth of her grandchild is shared by many grandmothers. The appearance of the new generation is like a promise of immortality. The family will go on, and there is no reason why the future should not be even better than the past—why this grandchild should not be the one to reach the goals that were only dreams to his parents and grandparents.

But the hopes are accompanied by anxious shadows of worry. Is the young mother mature enough for her new role? Will the young father be a good parent? What will the world be like when the new grandchild grows up? Will it be a happy place or a bleak, Orwellian desert?

Of course the prospective grandmother may find herself wondering and daydreaming long before the baby is born. What kind of grandmother will she be? Will she be a traditional grandmother who reads storybooks and rocks babies in a chair by the hearth? Will she have the best recipe for gingerbread, and will she know how to knit mittens and kiss away bumps and bruises? Will she be a source of tranquillity? A repository of the wisdom of age? Or will she be an exciting "Auntie Mame" sort of grandmother, laughing with her grandchild and bringing him into a world of delight and sophistication?

These questions will be answered in the future. The present is something else again. It can be a time for the grandmother to learn the shape and dimensions of this new role she will play—a role which can be so much more relaxed and relaxing than the role of mother, but which has its own limitations and restrictions.

Any grandmother has had many relationships before she comes to this one. She has been a friend, a lover, a parent, a wife. The feeling of expectation she experiences when she learns that she is going to be a grandmother may be familiar. Something new and exciting is going to happen. But the bond she will share with her grandchild is not like those other bonds—those which bind a woman to husband or friend, or to her own child.

The grandmother who is realistic knows that she will not play the primary role in guiding the development of the baby. The parenting will be done by the parents. But the grandmother can touch a child's life in ways that a parent cannot. She can enlarge the child's world and can share with the child a valuable perspective that will enrich his life. She can show the child where he is in the plan of things, and she can give the child a sense of permanence and stability. And of course she can be a bulwark of strength for the new parents.

As plans are made for the birth of the baby, most young parents realize that they will need help right after the baby is born.

Traditionally it is the maternal grandmother who comes to help. There is nothing cut and dried about human relationships, however, and sometimes the question of who will help is not easy to answer. The more sensitive the young parents are, the more difficult it can be.

Whenever this topic comes up, I think of Suzy, who called me when she was in her seventh month of pregnancy.

"We're having a hard time deciding which mother to ask to come stay with me after the baby is born," she said. "We love them both, and we don't want to hurt anyone's feelings."

"Don't you think you'd be more comfortable with your own mother?" I asked her. "After all, you're used to the way she does things."

"Well," said Suzy. That's all she said, and the way she said it should have been a warning. I was newer at my job of professional grandmother then, and I didn't pick up on it.

Suzy went to the hospital and had her baby. When she went home, the maternal grandmother was there loaded with gifts and glowing with delight. Three days later the maternal grandmother was on a plane home and Suzy and her husband were making do with the help of a local high school girl who came in every afternoon to make the beds, do the dishes, clean up the kitchen and help start dinner.

What went wrong?

"I was still my mother's little girl," said Suzy, when she came to see me after she had put the whole thing in perspective. "I hoped that maybe now that I have my own baby, my mother would stop babying me, but she didn't. The second I was home from the hospital I was being pampered and overprotected just the way I'd been when I was a teen. My mother wouldn't even let me hold the baby for fear he'd spit up on my pretty robe. She did everything for him, and I wasn't learning a thing about taking care of him and being a parent myself.

"Mother wasn't very nice to my husband, either. She treated him like the villain of the piece, and she hovered at me and kept talking about how I was supposed to 'recover' from my 'ordeal.' Two more weeks of that and Tom would have been suing for divorce—or maybe I would have. I'm tired now, but at least Tom and I are coping, and it's *our* baby, and Tom does not have to be a villain and I do not have to be a victim, and I suppose someday Mom will forgive me."

We can hope so, but after talking with a number

of new mothers like Suzy—mothers who experienced difficulties in those first scary days home from the hospital—I began to make a list of do's and don'ts for prospective grandmothers. The list has grown over the years and from time to time I change the rules for special circumstances, but it reads pretty much as follows:

Remember that the new mother is a grown-up, not a toddler who needs to be ordered around and sheltered from life.

Suzy's case, unfortunately, is typical of many where the maternal grandmother simply refused to give up her role of mother for the rewarding new one of grandmother. If you are going to have trouble recognizing the fact that your daughter can be a mother—and possibly a very good one—the warning signs will probably appear early in her pregnancy.

Are you sure that she isn't taking proper care of herself? Do you suspect that she doesn't know *how* to take care of herself? And that her husband doesn't know how to take care of her?

If you must answer yes to any of these questions, watch out. You could be a ringer for Suzy's mother—and you, too, could wind up on the plane three days after the new baby comes home from the hospital.

Don't try to compete with the other grandmother.

When Ruth's mother learned that Ruth and Dick

were going to be parents, she went immediately to the best department store in town and bought an almost complete layette.

Dick's mother, on the other hand, hurried to her neighborhood knit shop, bought yarn, and soon had an afghan for the carriage. She also made enough receiving blankets to accommodate half the population of Dayton, Ohio, in perfect comfort.

Ruth's mother bought a sterling silver baby mug and a silver photograph frame so that the new arrival could be framed in style once he was photographed.

Dick's mother took the basinet down from the attic. It was the family basinet which had been Dick's. She relined it with white satin and then sewed a new skirt for it—eyelet embroidery over satin, with ruffles and bows. It was as practical as a white velvet jump suit in a coal mine.

The baby arrived and both grandmothers descended on the young parents, bringing the layettes and the afghans and the sterling silver offerings.

The baby was cooed at and clucked over, and there was a grand competition in the kitchen to see who could bake the tastiest goodies for the new mother and who could heat the nursing bottles to exactly the right temperature. Neither of the grandmothers slept very much because the baby might wake up and need to be changed—which he did, regularly and often.

Ruth spent her first week at home without ever touching the baby except for the time she was actually nursing him. She suffered greatly from feelings of inadequacy, especially since either or both grandmothers were constantly present. If one grandmother wasn't crying, "Oh let me!" the other was saying, "It's no trouble! I was doing this before you were born!"

After that first week, the maternal grandmother went home to tend to her own dusty house and grumpy husband, who had been eating canned corned-beef hash the whole time. The paternal grandmother took a plane back to San Francisco to tend to her job.

Ruth and Dick carried the baby home from the airport and immediately knew that they had to change a diaper.

"I did it," said Ruth, "and Dick helped, and when it was done we were both so exhausted we had to sit down and Dick had a drink. Then we started to laugh—it was so dumb. We're okay now, but it's a good thing it only lasted for a week. If it had gone on much longer, we'd have been paralyzed."

Of course they would have been paralyzed—and the baby would have been spoiled.

Whenever I hear that both grandmothers are

coming to help with the new baby, I do all that I can to discourage it. No matter how well the two women get along under normal circumstances, both should not arrive at the same time for an extended stay with the new baby and the young parents. Rivalry will almost surely spring up, and the young parents will be frustrated, uneasy and probably apprehensive when they should be concentrating on being—and becoming—parents.

And the baby?

Well, any baby who has to entertain two grandmas, both of whom want equal time, is working harder than a baby should when he's so brand new.

If two grandmothers insist on being helpful, I usually suggest that the visits run consecutively. The maternal grandmother usually is there when the new mother first comes home from the hospital. However, there could be many reasons for the paternal grandmother to arrive first. If the grandmothers have worked things out sensibly, one of them stays with the young couple for a week or so. She does not try to make an indelible impression on the new baby, who won't remember anything about it anyway. Instead, she does what she can to keep the house running smoothly while the new mother looks after the baby. In due time she leaves the young family to be on their own for a few days. Then, before the young mother can be overwhelmed by the constant demands of the baby, the second grandmother arrives. She is usually welcomed with open arms, and her visit gives the young parents time to get away by themselves for a few hours.

The prospective grandmother may need to remember that the new parents are another generation. They may have a different lifestyle. They are entitled to that lifestyle.

My telephone rang one afternoon and I picked up the receiver to hear sobbing on the other end. It was Renee, who had been in my prenatal class. She had given birth to Jeffrey ten days earlier. He was a fine, healthy baby. She had been happy and her husband, Bob, had been proud the day the two had taken him home. I had received one call from Renee about a diaper rash and then had heard nothing further. Now Renee was on the telephone weeping great salt tears and hiccuping as she said incoherent things about somebody's mother.

It took Renee a few minutes to calm down. Then she told me what the trouble was—and the trouble was with *her* mother.

"She came the day we got home from the hospital," said Renee, "and she doesn't approve of me! My own mother doesn't approve of me! She says I'm spoiled and selfish. She says Bob is a lousy father. He just took her to the airport. I don't think she'll ever speak to me again! I don't know how I could have done such a thing!"

As it turned out, what Renee had done was to play some music on the stereo. Actually, she had played rather a lot of music on the stereo, since both she and Bob were jazz fans.

Renee and Bob had not embarked on their home jazz festival without proper forethought. When they had talked to the pediatrician during their prenatal visit, they had asked if the music would bother the baby.

"I'm going to take it for granted that you aren't talking about music that's turned up to a volume that makes the walls vibrate," said the pediatrician. "No fair shattering the baby's eardrums. But if it's not too loud, definitely the music won't hurt a thing. A newborn should get used to the regular household noises—vacuum cleaners, barking dogs, and music too. It isn't necessary to tip-toe around just because you've got a baby in the house."

So Renee and Bob had played their music. And what had Renee's mother done when she arrived? She had tip-toed. She had shushed Bob and Renee, and she had strongly indicated that visitors should talk in whispers, if at all. Needless to say, she had taken strong exception to the music the young parents both loved. Although Jeffrey was a good baby, he did cry now and then. Whenever he cried, Grandma would say, "No wonder! That crazy music is upsetting him!"

"We tried to cool it," said Renee. "We figured Mother wasn't going to be around forever, and we could play the stereo later when she was gone.

Then Bob brought home a new recording and we wanted to try it, and when Jeffrey woke up from his nap he started to cry."

"He wanted to let you know he was awake," I told Renee.

"Well sure," said Renee. "He always cries when he wakes up. But Mother marched into the room and she said, 'That music goes or I go!' Well, we'd been trying so hard, and we both got mad. I saw Bob turn red, like he was going to choke. And before I could think about it, I said, 'Okay. You go.'"

It was unfortunate. It shouldn't have happened. If the new grandmother had taken up her role with a live-and-let-live attitude, it wouldn't have happened.

Which brings us to the next rule:

Remember that you will be a guest in the home of your daughter or daughter-in-law—or she will be a guest in your home.

Plan to show the young parents the same courtesy you would show a stranger. The first days home from the hospital can be a time of sharing, learning and serenity, rather than an ordeal to be survived.

Bear in mind that you do not necessarily have two strikes on you if the new mother is a daughter-in-law.

Sometimes it is the paternal grandmother who lives nearby or who has the time to give when the new baby comes home.

In my experience, mothers-in-law are far more loved and accepted than one would believe after hearing all the jokes. In many cases the mother-in-law and the young wife are close friends. Sometimes the young wife feels intimidated by her own mother and will turn to her mother-in-law when she has problems.

If you have not already established a good rapport with your daughter-in-law, the advent of your first grandchild will be an ideal time to begin. But examine your own attitudes with scrupulous honesty. When there is a problem with the in-law relationship, it usually arises from jealousy. Have you been overprotective of your son? Do you feel that his new wife isn't really good enough for him? Deep down in your heart, do you object to sharing his love with this young woman—this outsider?

If you detect even a trace of these attitudes in yourself, get busy. Look for things to like about your daughter-in-law. Even if she doesn't do things quite the way you do, keep an open mind. There are probably rituals and customs she learned from her mother that she is comfortable with. You may be wiser and happier if you respect them. Remember that we are never too old to learn new things.

Remember also to tell your son's wife occasionally that something she has done, or some new thing she thought of, was a good idea.

Sometimes there are conflicts in families and they can't be resolved. If this is the case, it would be madness to try to help the young mother when she brings the baby home. Other arrangements will have to be made, but do try to keep the lines of communication open. If you are not able to be friends, there is no need to be enemies. You don't want to lose contact with your grandchild, who will always be a part of your family—and an extension of yourself.

Of course you're going to love your new grandchild. Babies are easy to love. But you had better give first consideration to the new mother. She is the one who needs help.

"My mother was the perfect grandmother," Cindy told me. "I took care of the baby and she ran the support system. She did the shopping and the cooking and she kept the house going. She also made me feel pretty special. It even beats cooking to have somebody with you who's warm and affectionate and supportive."

That pretty well sums up what you're planning to do, and if you can do it without upsetting the household or forcing your ways onto the young couple, so much the better.

Be flexible.

If you have no other demands on your time— and the expectant parents agree—you may decide to arrive a week or so before the baby is due. You will have a chance to visit, to help with the last-minute preparations and to get the feel of the household.

If this is not a practical idea, you may want to set things up so that you can arrive after labor has begun or after the baby has been born. Keep in mind the fact that very few babies arrive on the day they are due. Sometimes they come weeks ahead of time. Often they are late. More than one prospective grandmother has arrived on the date the baby was due and then had to leave before the birth, or before the baby came home from the hospital, to get back to a job.

Whether the baby is early or late, and whether you are a lady with unlimited time or a busy career woman, it is the attitudes you will bring to your new role as grandmother that will set the stage for a lifetime of family sharing. Three generations— parents, child and grandparents—all have their unique gifts to contribute. As time passes the relationships and interactions in the new family system will change and that is as it should be. With a good start, the chances are that the changes will be healthy ones and that the family will grow ever stronger.

THE MORE THINGS CHANGE,
THE MORE THEY STAY
THE SAME

Even though it has been years since Grandmother handled a baby, chances are she isn't going to feel strange with the newborn. Babies still cry, sneeze, have hiccups, spit up, and wet with great regularity. If they are healthy, not much is apt to go wrong. They are tolerant and permissive, moreover, and will not even notice if the new grandmother who picks them up is a bit clumsy, or if she doesn't diaper them correctly.

Of course handling a baby is a knack, and if Grandma is relaxed she will soon have it again, just as she once had it. She will help the new mother relax too.

But if babies don't change, child-rearing methods do. To avoid shock, bewilderment and outrage, the new grandmother may want to bring herself up to date on the new ways *before* she gets into an argument with the new parents.

For example:

Germs are no longer terribly scary.

Today's grandmother has vivid memories of hours spent sterilizing bottles and nipples. She remembers the fear that the nipple would be contaminated by handling as she tried to put it onto the bottle. Today it is hard to explain what the big worry was all about. Babies are not that fragile and even the most tenderly cared for child has come into contact with billions of germs by the time it's a few hours old.

Do not give vent to any little screams of fright and horror when you see your newborn grandchild being fed cold milk from a nursing bottle which has just been taken from the refrigerator. It is all right! Most pediatricians approve! Most pediatricians also approve of the fact that the nursing bottle has not been sterilized. Nowadays hot sudsy water is all that is needed to wash nursing bottles. After they are washed they are rinsed well, or put through a cycle in the electric dishwasher. The formula goes in after the dishwasher has completed its performance. The bottles go into the refrigerator and the new mother is all set.

Disposable diapers are just as respectable as the other kind.

The very first time I was asked to baby-sit with my new grandchild, the parents arrived with a box of paper diapers. I was horrified. Like the grandmother in the television commercial, I was sure that a "good" mother always used cloth diapers. I said as much.

The new parents left, taking the baby, and the paper diapers, with them.

It was one of my bigger mistakes. I was stubborn about it, too. I wanted to prove my point and I wanted to make sure my grandchild was being treated properly. So I did a study of babies who were diapered with paper and compared them to babies who were diapered with cloth.

There was no difference between the two groups of babies. Paper absorbs as well as cloth and babies are notoriously indifferent about what is wrapped around their bottoms. The parents will probably decide about paper versus cloth depending on their lifestyle, and there is no need for the new grandmother even to comment on their decision.

Pacifiers will not disfigure a child for life, and they are not likely to destroy his character.

When we were bringing up our children, pacifiers were taboo. It was widely believed that a baby who was permitted to use a pacifier would end up with a malformed mouth. Pacifiers were also supposed to lead to infections, since once the baby began to suck on one, it could not be kept sterile.

Today the thinking about pacifiers has changed. Some pediatricians still resolutely disapprove of them, but many doctors feel that babies need extra sucking. "If we don't allow a baby a pacifier," says one pediatrician, "he may find his thumb. Thumb-sucking *can* lead to malformations of the jaw. Also, when the sucking instinct diminishes at about six months of age, it is not difficult to take a pacifier away from the baby. It is impossible to take away his thumb."

To use a pacifier or not to use one is a choice that new parents will make with the baby's doctor. Like the choice between paper diapers and cloth, it can pass without comment from the grandmother.

Unless they are actually going to journey to the Arctic, babies do not need to be bundled too warmly.

With my first grandchild, I made the mistake of overbundling. I was keeping the baby overnight for the first time and I was in a frenzy of carefulness. I had kept a nice woolen baby blanket down through the years and I saw to it that the baby was swaddled securely in it so that no stray draft could chill her. I also saw to it that the room where she slept was nice and warm.

The baby wakened in the night crying and I found her bathed in perspiration from head to foot.

I changed her and held her, and when she went back to sleep I covered her with a lighter blanket. When the new parents came for her the next day, I casually asked whether they kept her room nice and warm when they put her down to sleep.

"No," said the young mother, "not especially. She gets along the way we do—with the room at the same temperature as ours. The pediatrician says it isn't good to keep her room too warm or to overbundle her. The books all say the same thing."

Baby carriages aren't what they used to be, and some-times cribs are different, too.

The umbrella stroller is the new mode of trans-portation for the baby. It is made of a light, soft fabric and it has a frame that folds easily. Umbrella strollers are much handier for parents than the old cumbersome carriages, and even if they look flimsy to you, you need not worry, as I did, about their giving adequate support to the baby's back. All the doctors I work with have assured me that they're fine.

Cribs and basinets are not necessarily the same these days. Today some parents—and some grandparents—have splurged and gotten the new babies heated water cribs or basinets with water mattresses. Babies can only be bundled for a month or so; after that they may have a tendency to kick off the covers when they are left in the crib. With a heated water mattress there is no worry about the baby becoming chilled. He will be warm and cozy even without a blanket covering him. Also the warmth and motion of the mattress can be very soothing.

The front-pack carrier is another innovation. When this is used, the baby is carried comfortably in front of the mother. Children thrive on the warmth and security as they cuddle against the mother. Then, when they get older, they may graduate to backpacks which give them a chance to look out at the world over Daddy's or Mommy's shoulder.

A wonderful gift for Grandmother to give the baby is the automatic swing. This can be a godsend for the young mother after Grandmother leaves. The baby can sit in a comfortable seat while the swing is wound up so that it moves gently back and forth. The swing will work for fifteen minutes or so, keeping the baby happy and amused while Mother tends to other things.

The baby swing may seem like quite a sophisticated present for a child, but most babies are ready to use one when they are only three weeks of age.

Babies don't need solids right away.

When our children were born there was often competition among the new mothers about the variety of solid foods their babies could consume.

"Johnny had cereal at three weeks," one young mother might say.

The young mother would then be topped by a friend who started her infant on vegetables at two weeks. The really gifted baby ate more solids earlier than the other newborns in the neighborhood. There was something virtuous about persuading a tiny baby to eat applesauce. It was on a par with entering him at Harvard the day he was born.

Today most pediatricians suggest that mothers put off giving the baby solid food for four to six months. There are two reasons for this: first, a baby will get all the nourishment his body needs from the milk he is taking. Secondly, the pediatricians believe that if solids are offered too early, there is a greater chance that the baby will develop problems with allergies.

In the matter of nourishment, be guided by the new mother, who is surely being guided by the pediatrician. And never, never tell the new parents that the baby wouldn't cry so much if he was getting enough to eat!

Any mention of food immediately brings us to the subject of breast-feeding.

This is the area of child care where there is the greatest conflict between new parents and grandmothers.

When we had our children, formula feeding was almost the rule. Those of us who did breast-feed enjoyed two advantages: we stayed in the hospital longer, since breast milk generally comes in on the third or fourth day. Then, when we went home, our milk and feeding schedules were established—and once we were at home we had the support of mothers and grandmothers who had successfully breast-fed.

Many new mothers today leave the hospital before their milk is in. A schedule is hard to establish during the first days home, so the poor mother seems to be nursing all the time. Also, breasts are not like bottles. It is hard for the nursing mother to be sure how much milk the baby is getting.

With breast-feeding, as with most other areas of

child care, the mother and the grandmother need to be relaxed. Anxiety is the big enemy. It may be difficult for the grandmother to hear her new grandchild crying, and even more difficult for her to keep from telling the mother that she doesn't have enough milk.

Remember that only a very small percentage of healthy mothers cannot breast-feed. All the mother needs if she is to be successful is encouragement— lots of it! Bring her plenty of fluids (ten to twelve glasses a day), make sure she's eating a balanced diet, reassure her and love her, and you will have a healthy, well-nourished grandchild.

A bath is a bath is a bath.

Not much has changed since you bathed your own babies, except that today more and more fathers are getting into the sudsy water up to their elbows.

New parents are more flexible today about how often the baby is bathed and about the time of the bath. It need not necessarily be in the morning. Child care is more casual now and often more comfortable. Many fathers have attended prenatal classes and learned how to care for their babies. However, most young men still harbor a secret fear that the baby will break if he isn't held correctly and they are delighted to have a grandmother on hand for assurance during the first few baths.

In helping bathe the baby, as in everything you do for the young parents, reassurance is the key word. You are there to encourage, not to take over. In time, the young couple will be on their own with the baby. It will be your main concern to help them get there easily and soon.

THE NEW FAMILY

At the beginning of this century, almost all babies were born at home. Then, in the years between 1910 and 1920, women began to go to hospitals to give birth. The hospital was considered the safest place for both the mother and the child. It still is.

With the majority of births taking place in hospitals, the mortality rate went down dramatically. However, there were many things about the hospital experience that were depressing and even dehumanizing.

Many young mothers felt that they ceased to be people when they were subjected to the hospital routine. They were no longer surrounded by family. Since it wasn't "sterile" to have anyone other than hospital personnel in the labor room or the delivery room, even the husbands could not be there to encourage and support the mothers. When she was actually about to give birth, the mother was sedated so completely that she was really not present when her child first appeared in the world.

She recovered consciousness after it was all over. Usually she was back in her room, and the nurse was bringing in the new baby—wrapped and swaddled and red-faced with outrage—so that the mother could have a peek at him and be assured that she had indeed had a child.

In this arrangement, fathers were tolerated to a certain degree. They were informed when the baby was safely born and they were told the sex of the child. After the birth they were allowed to visit the mother at designated hours. They were almost never allowed to hold the baby. Instead they looked at the child through the glass window of the nursery.

The mother stayed in the hospital for a week or more, and the baby was brought in to be fed every four hours. When it was time for the mother to go home, her child was still a stranger.

Clinically, the iron routine of the maternity ward was fine. Psychologically, it was all wrong. In time we learned that expectant mothers need the support of loved ones during labor and delivery. Husbands need to feel needed during this important time. And babies need to bond with their parents.

A bond is something that binds things together, that unites individuals into a group. The word "bonding" became very popular during the sixties and seventies to describe a thing that took place easily and naturally when the birth occurred at home. It is the process by which the child becomes a part of the family and learns to recognize the parents who nourish him and care for him. The child also becomes part of a group which can include grandparents, aunts, uncles and siblings. Until recently, however, the baby who was born in a hospital setting had very little chance to know the people who would be most important in his life. His contacts with his mother were fragmentary, and his father did not even exist for him until he was a week old. Siblings, grandparents and other family members did not appear on the scene at all.

Gradually the family, the doctors and the nurses came to realize that this needed to be changed. The old hard-line, inflexible routine of the maternity ward was changed, so today parents-to-be share the whole birth experience. The mother is not deposited in a labor room by herself. Instead, the father is with her, helping time the contractions, comforting and encouraging.

When the birth is imminent, the mother is not nearly as sedated as she would have been twenty years ago. Sometimes, if she has had LaMaze classes and has done her breathing exercises, she is not sedated at all. She is not an inert object during the birth. She is working and cooperating and she sees her baby the moment it is born. She holds the child even before the cord is cut, and if the father is in the delivery room (as he often is) he holds the baby, too. Bonding begins to take place.

The newborn is often amazingly alert during the first hour after birth and good eye-to-eye contact takes place. Usually the baby goes into a deep sleep after that first hour. He may sleep for eight to sixteen hours and the mother has a chance to rest.

Rooming-in is available in most hospitals today. When the new family chooses rooming-in, the baby stays with the mother. Mother, father and baby have a chance to be together during much of the hospital stay. The rigid four-hour feeding schedules have been abolished and the newborns are fed on reasonable demand.

In some hospitals the extended family, and not only the parents, shares in the birth experience. It is certainly not practical to have uncles, aunts, siblings, cousins and mothers-in-law present in the delivery room. However, parents who want the warmth and support of other family members can elect to use a facility in some hospitals which is called the alternative birth center because it is an alternative to having the baby at home.

The alternative birth center, or ABC, looks like an ordinary bedroom in an ordinary home. It contains a bed which does not resemble a hospital bed, comfortable chairs for several people and usually a television set. The mother who plans to give birth in this room must take special classes. Then, when it is time for her baby to arrive, she comes into the hospital. She is not put into a labor room, moved to a delivery room and then put into a recovery room. Instead she stays in the bed in the ABC, just as she would stay in her own bed if she were giving birth at home. Family members and friends witness the birth and share the joy with the new family.

In an alternative birth center, the grandmother can be part of the experience, *if she desires!* And if the parents are willing. There is nothing obligatory about this. If the grandmother chooses to stay at home dusting the nursery furniture and the mother decides to confine the witnesses to the doctor, nurses and her husband, her decision will be respected. Childbirth should be a joyful time, not an occasion that requires extraordinary displays of bravery.

Whether you witness the birth or not, you will have to recognize the fact that your child has become a parent. Nothing will ever be the same. It may help to think back to the first time you became a parent and to remember the many important changes which occurred in your life and your husband's. It was a time of great adjustment for you; it will be the same for your child. Perhaps the new mother and father will be a bit frightened and uncertain. If so, the new grandmother can give them encouragement and praise, helping them feel comfortable in their new roles.

The grandmother who is wise will try to do this without making the young people feel inadequate. They are probably going to feel slightly inadequate at first in any event, but if the grandmother tries to take over—to show how well *she* can change a diaper or burp the baby—the young mother may respond with the resentment a child feels toward an overbearing mother. If you plan to be a truly beloved grandmother, it is important to realize that your help is greatly needed—and that it must be tempered with wisdom and moderation.

Again, a few rules may guide you in helping the new family in the easiest way.

First, before you define your role, talk things over with the other members of the cast.

If you can, spend some time chatting with the young parents *before* the baby comes. Find out about areas where you can be most helpful.

Your primary goal will probably be to keep the household running smoothly while the young parents become better acquainted with the baby. Although today's grandmother is frequently a career woman, she can bring her own brand of creativity to this task.

Creativity does not imply rearranging the living room furniture or painting the second bathroom. The less uproar at this time the better. The new parents have plenty of changes to cope with without having their surroundings tampered with. But the new grandmother may want to cook special dishes and serve them attractively. She may think of delightful ways to make the new mother feel treasured and appreciated.

"I really missed my mom after she left," Wendy told me. "The first few days I was home from the hospital, she would make my bed up fresh while I took my shower, and she'd always have a clean nightgown ready for me. We kept the baby with us in our room, and every night my mother made up a 'night pack' for us. There was a change of clothes in it, and diapers and disposable wash cloths. I didn't even have to get out of bed to change the baby when she woke up for feeding."

A "night pack" is a marvelous idea. And what new mother won't appreciate a special comfortable corner where she can feed the baby? This can be arranged with a rocking chair, if one is available, or simply a chair that the mother will find comfortable as she sits with the baby in her arms. There should be a soft light, a table to hold a glass of juice or milk, if the mother is nursing, and a nursing bottle if she is not. Don't forget the cloth the mother will need when she burps the baby.

You might suggest that you be the one to answer the telephone while the new mother is resting, or while she is feeding the baby. Have a pad and pencil handy to take messages.

You might ask if there is any ironing to do. Even in this age of dacrons and nylons, most households have a small heap of ironing hidden away in a drawer or on a closet shelf. The young mother might be glad to know that this is being taken care of.

Are you an expert needlewoman? You might ask about mending that needs to be done, or hems that could be taken up or let down. Now that the baby is on the scene clamoring for attention, the young mother will not have much time for this sort of thing.

Is baking your forte? What could be nicer or more cozy for new parents than to cuddle with the baby as the aroma of homemade cookies wafts from the kitchen?

I am sure most grandmothers will think of many other nice things to do. Go to it, but do check with the new parents before you undertake anything that could be considered a reorganization.

If the young parents seem afraid of the baby, or harried, or even resentful, do not be upset.

Parental love may not spring forth at the moment of birth. Sometimes it takes a while. Babies are very small and often, when they are very new, are unattractive.

"Bill looked like a monkey!" said one young mother. "I worked like a horse to get him born, and that's the way he paid me back. Red in the face, too, and he yelled thirty-two hours a day."

"Long day," I said.

"You'd better believe it," said the young mother.

Most young women are not this forthright. If they are disappointed in their babies, or if they do not experience a warm rush of maternal feeling when they hold the newborns, they may become quiet. They may withdraw and brood.

These mothers are not "unnatural." The maternal feelings will come. Perhaps the young mother will not feel the blissful ecstasy that one reads about in books and on greeting cards, but the young mother will love her baby, and the child who looks like a monkey (or a tadpole—lots of babies resemble tadpoles) will shape up, lose his magenta tint and eventually grow hair. It just takes a little while.

Paternal emotions may be even longer in asserting themselves. The new father has not actually given birth. He is usually gone all day and he may not feel that the new little human being on the scene is real, or that the baby is now a permanent part of his life. Give daddy a little space and he'll come around.

Even if you're looking after the household, you don't need to be there nonstop.

Keep your sensitivity working; you may get the message now and then that the new family needs to be alone together for a little while.

Feelings of rejection are not becoming or appropriate at this point. It doesn't matter if you have traveled across the country to be with your daughter. It doesn't matter if you have slogged through snowdrifts to get to the hospital. If the new mother and daddy want to be alone with their baby—or just with each other—they have that privilege.

They are entitled to privacy. They should be permitted to say things that no one else overhears— not even the grandmother.

If there is a dog, you might want to take him for a walk. If there is no dog, offer to do some marketing. You can always pick up some favorite fruit juices which will be important for the nursing mother. You can always get some fresh air; fresh air is good for everyone. None of us ever has enough.

Enjoy yourself, and don't be afraid of touching.

Two of the saddest people I have ever known are Charles and Jonathan, who were born to a registered nurse during that bleak period in our history when babies were not supposed to be touched. In addition to being a firm believer in non-touching, Margaret, their mother, was terrified of germs. Her boys were hygienically raised. They were not cuddled, since cuddling would spoil the boys and would also lead to an unhealthy exchange of germs between mother and child.

Everything they came into contact with was kept sterile until they were a year old. Even after that, there was very little of the normal give and take that happens with youngsters. Charles never got a lick of Jonathan's lollipop and Jonathan did not drink out of Charles' toothbrush glass.

The boys were fed on a schedule as strict as that in any hospital. They were not picked up when they cried, but were left to "cry it out."

When they were older—but not too old—they were given a thorough grounding in the facts of life. One suspects that this hygienic approach carried over into this part of their education. Their mother explained the entire matter in terms of fish and farm animals, taking them on several visits to model dairies and at least one pig farm. She explained that sex was perfectly normal and natural and that all creatures did it, and of course she hoped that they would not become curious and take to experimenting when they reached their teens and possibly get into trouble.

The boys grew, flourished, were chock full of vitamins, had straight teeth and exercised regularly. They did not get into trouble with sex in their teens, possibly because too much hygiene can take the romance out of anything.

Charles became a tennis instructor and now holds forth in Phoenix and has been unable to form a lasting attachment with any lady. He sees his mother once every year or two. She cannot understand how he can neglect her so. She took such good care of him when he was small.

Jonathan married, had one child, then found the closeness of the connubial bond almost suffocating. There were no more children and Jonathan now lives in an apartment over the garage. He has his own television set there, a photographic darkroom and a fine collection of tapes and records.

The moral is clear. In this case, total sterility can

lead to a life of total sterility, and touching is a good thing. The more a baby is touched and fondled, the more he will respond. New babies do not understand speech and their eyes do not focus, so at first they won't learn by listening or looking. But even when they are very tiny, they are learning by touching and by being touched.

The infant will know his mother's gentle caress before he is many days old. He will feel his daddy lift him in strong, caring hands. He will get to know his grandmother who tends him with confidence and love.

As the child grows, he will become a lap baby if he is lucky, and a warm hug, a squeeze or a kiss will be a positive input for him.

The art of touching does not come easily to some people, but it is never too late to discover the miracles it can produce. If you haven't touched a child lately, what better time to do so than now, as a new family begins? Touch is a very important expression of love and the very best grandchildren are the ones who aren't afraid to love.

The new parents don't need to be left out either. The mother has done well. Why shouldn't she respond to an affectionate kiss? And why shouldn't the daddy enjoy a nice hug? Most people do.

Give advice only when you're asked.

Of course you are on the scene to help, but the help you give need not necessarily be verbalized. Remember that new parents are overwhelmed with advice. When it comes to babies, everyone is an expert. Everyone has either had a baby or been one. Neighbors, friends, doctors and nurses all tell the uncertain new mother and the intimidated father what to do..

It's natural that every grandmother will have definite ideas on how to raise the baby, but remember that most young parents lack assurance at first. Like anyone in a new job, they are touchy about criticism. As they gain confidence, this will pass. When they feel more comfortable asking for and receiving advice, you won't have to exercise your iron will quite so much. In the meantime, let the new parents know that you'll be glad to tell them anything you can—anything they want to know that you *do* know—but that until they ask, you'll hold your tongue.

When they do ask, give the most considered and considerate opinion you can, one that is untinged by criticism.

Phrases to be avoided at all costs are, "Well, if it was my baby . . ." and "Honey, I hate to find fault, but . . ." and "I was wondering when you'd notice *that?*"

Don't be afraid to say that you don't know.

Part of the grandmother's "image" has to do with expertise. The grandmother likes to feel that she can hear a baby cry in the night and know instantly why he is crying. She can also change diapers in the dark, burp the baby more satisfactorily than the most experienced baby nurse and deal with colic or diaper rash more easily than the best pediatrician.

Some grandmothers are indeed this efficient, but the best grandmothers, like the best friends, occasionally don't know all the answers and aren't afraid to say so.

I think fondly of Alice, who called one day to ask a question about her eight-day-old son, Eric.

"I don't know," said Alice, "and my mom doesn't know either, and maybe you know."

Then Alice chuckled. "It was okay to hear Mom say she doesn't know. I used to think she was supermom and I could never measure up—you know, never be as good as she is. But if she doesn't know, it's okay for me not to know, isn't it?"

Alice's reaction was predictable. After a baby is born, new parents often feel a strong closeness to their own parents. They realize that it isn't easy to be a parent and they begin to appreciate the time, effort and caring that they received from their mothers and fathers. They resolve to do as well for their own child, and if grandmother has not overawed them with her perfection, they can face the task without being intimidated by it.

Make allowances for "baby blues."

A young mother can be terrified by the thought of being responsible for a tiny infant. At the same time, when the baby is new, she is trying to adjust to changes which have occurred and which are occurring in her system. She may be exhausted from nights spent listening tensely for the baby to cry—and worrying when the baby doesn't cry.

The old wives used to say that a new mother was "not herself." Indeed, she may be as unlike herself as a changeling. She may be depressed and cranky, lashing out for no apparent reason. If Grandmother is nearby, she may be on the receiving end of the squall.

New mothers are not only easily irritated, they are also fiercely protective of their babies. There appears to be an almost biological instinct that dictates possessive behavior on the part of the mother. It made more sense when mankind lived in caves and the new mother had to protect her infant from marauding animals. Today we don't have that problem, but the instinct remains. It manifests itself in a need to feel in charge of the new family. It is important for the grandmother to let the mother be in control of her house and husband, and certainly of her child. Try to hold your tongue during this uncomfortable period and remember that your daughter does not really hate you or anyone else. Don't take it personally. This, too, will pass.

Usually the baby blues disappear as soon as the new mother gets a good night's sleep. They may return again if a light bulb burns out or a dish breaks. However, if the people around the mother are supportive, and the new baby is not too demanding, the depression and the fits of temper should be gone within a month.

The baby's temperament plays a big part in determining how well and how soon the new mother will adjust to her role and become her usual pleasant, well-mannered self. Some babies are placid and their mothers should be eternally grateful, but some babies are "screamers."

If the new baby is a screamer, the new mommy and daddy will be sure they are doing something wrong. They will be tired and on edge anyway and the new mother will doubtless be on the verge of tears most of the time. Countless telephone calls will be made to the pediatrician.

Once you have ascertained that there really is nothing wrong—that the new arrival is just exercising his lungs and making his presence felt—the only thing you can do is assure the new parents that it isn't his fault. The baby is crying because he needs to cry and this fact has nothing to do with the way they changed his diaper or gave the bath.

Don't ever compare a fussy grandchild to your own "good" children. Don't ever tell a young mother that her husband slept peacefully through the night when he was only three weeks old. Don't ever imply that the fretful baby must get his tendency to wail and weep from "the other side of the family."

First of all, having a "good" child is something

for which you can't take credit. It is as accidental as having a child with red hair or small feet. Secondly, the chances that your children were quite that "good" are small. Once a child is grown we tend to forget the sleepless nights and the mornings filled with uproar, just as we tend to forget the labor pains. We only rejoice that a child was born into the world and—miracle of miracles—he or she finally grew up!

Neatness doesn't necessarily count.

If the young parents live in a house that is a bit untidy, they probably are more comfortable that way. Trying to bring perfect order to an extremely casual house could easily be construed as criticism. Besides, you were invited to share this important time with the new family because they love you—not because you're such a whiz with the vacuum cleaner. The new parents would much prefer that you give them the gift of your company and that you be relaxed and at ease with the new baby. That's what grandmothers are about. A sparkling, magazine-perfect home isn't important. Loving and sharing are.

Give Daddy T.L.C., too.

Before the birth, daddy probably played a major role in getting ready for the baby. He may have done a lot of handholding and helping out with the chores. He probably went shopping or pushed a vacuum when his wife, tired and feeling fat, needed lots of emotional support and assistance.

Many dads today attend weekly prenatal classes with their wives to prepare for their new responsibilities. Young fathers learn relaxation techniques, so that at the time of labor they can help their wives. They are often there in the delivery room, coaching and cheerleading, helping the mother to relax without a lot of medication.

After months of being almost an equal partner in the pregnancy, it can be quite a letdown for daddy to come home and find that he is not as important in the daily routine as he once was. Mother and the baby are the center of attention. Flowers arrive, the telephone rings, people come to call and mother is told how beautiful she looks, and how delightful the baby is. Dad takes a back seat.

You can do a lot to make it better. First of all, don't ignore the young father. Make sure he knows that he is as important now as he was before the baby was born. Encourage him to help care for the baby. If he needs it, give moral support as he bathes or diapers.

Remember, no matter how many classes he has attended, the baby he is handling now is his very own. Young fathers may like to pretend that they are cool, but most share a common fear: they think they may hurt the baby if they don't handle him exactly right.

"I wish someone had told me ahead of time that babies don't break," said one young man. "I was sure if I held my daughter close to me the way I wanted to, I'd snap her arm or a leg."

Assure the young father that the baby's little bones are still soft and almost unbreakable. The baby's skin will not tear if Daddy washes the baby's face. And Daddy's big hands and strong arms will make the baby feel very safe and secure.

When he is through with the bathing, diapering, or swaddling of the baby in a receiving blanket as they do in the hospital nursery, you might pamper daddy and bring a pillow to prop his head. Or just give him an appreciative pat. He's tired, too.

Things get even better the second time around.

I have heard many grandmothers say they could never love another grandchild as they did the first. I felt that way myself before my second, third and fourth grandchild arrived, but I have found that there is never a shortage of space in the human heart. It can always grow to encompass another love.

Grandma will be needed when the second child is brought home from the hospital. Perhaps her presence will be even more vital than it was with the first baby. If the mother is breast feeding, she will have to devote much time to the new baby. Then a loving grandmother will give much-needed assurance to the older child.

The household will be much more relaxed after the second baby. The parents will have more confidence and will feel easier about asking questions. They will be glad of the love you are giving to the older child and so will you. Grandmothers are supposed to have fun and there are few things more fun than playing with a favorite grandchild and letting him know you think he's simply grand!

Things can be even easier at Grandmother's house.

If Grandma lives close enough and there is room for the new family, the young parents and the newborn may go to the grandmother's house for the first week or so after they leave the hospital. This arrangement can work out very well.

When the young people are guests in your home, it is easier and more natural for you to assume the kitchen duties. Since you know where things are, you don't need to worry about upsetting someone else's arrangements as you go about preparing meals and looking after the house. Also, you will sleep better in your bed, and thus will be more rested when you deal with the daytime chores. The new mother may also rest better when she does not have to concern herself with what's going on in the household.

The new grandmother who is helping to care for the baby in her own home has one temptation, however. She may want to show off her grandchild to her friends. Remember that the fewer people the new parents have to see in the first week or so, the better. They are both weary. Just take this time to get to know your new pride and joy.

After a few weeks, everyone will be ready to meet the public.

When it's time to go, don't linger in the doorway.

Leaving the new family, or having them leave you, will not be easy. All grandmothers feel that the days pass too quickly and with each day the attachment to that wonderful new person in the basinet becomes stronger. Grandmother can look at the baby and see gestures that are strangely familiar. The baby is a further extension of a loved husband, or of the grandmother herself. The grandmother may want to stay indefinitely to watch the little personality unfold. The grand-mother who gives in to this temptation is just asking for trouble.

Remember that you have your own life to go back to. If you go back to it at the time you and the new parents have agreed, you can look forward to years which will be enriched by the new child. Grandmothers may take a special interest in toy shops and children's games. Many grandmothers will enjoy hearing news regarding weight gains, the first smile; the first tooth and the first word. The pictures will come in the mail, or if you live near the young family they may be hand delivered. The child will continue to be a part of you, even though someone else is caring for his needs on a day-to-day basis.

Leaving will not be easy. The time may have gone too quickly. You may have doubts about how well the young mother has regained her strength. However, unless something unexpected has happened, leave on schedule. Remember what they say about fish and houseguests. Go. The new family needs to get on with their new life and you need to get on with the one you've been leading all along.

THE BEST IS YET
TO COME

"No matter how many communes anybody invents," said anthropologist Margaret Mead, "the family always creeps back."

Lifestyles have changed since we had our own families. However, grandmothers have not become obsolete. They are needed now more than ever. In today's nuclear family, grandmothers can provide stability, continuity and tradition. And of course once she is a grandmother, a woman will be a grandmother forever. She will continue to have a place in the family even after the new mother has fully recovered her strength and even after the child is grown.

Most grandmothers want above all to be close to their children and their grandchildren. It is not always easy for us to accept a new lifestyle, however. We may find it difficult to maintain a loving, nonjudgmental attitude when we see our children doing things we wouldn't have considered at their age—or at any age! But if we are going to be generous in our loving, we must be tolerant of different values and different styles. The prayer for serenity might have been written for today's grandmothers:

"God grant me the serenity to accept the things I cannot change, the courage to change the things I can, and the wisdom to know the difference."

Even if we think something can be changed, it is important to be practical as well as wise and to put up a fight only for those principles we feel are absolutely vital.

Although they may reject our values, our children do not want us to reject them. They need our support and love. And as time goes by, we will find that there is no generation gap between ourselves and our grandchildren. We understand each other perfectly.

After the infancy is over, the true delights of being a grandmother unfold. You will find yourself sharing good times with the baby. You will begin to play again and you'll discover a new sense of adventure.

You don't have to discipline your grandchild; your special times with him are for fun. Mother and Dad may occasionally have to be stern, but you can just enjoy the child's company.

Grandchildren are for spoiling, just a bit, and it is a rare child indeed who doesn't appreciate being spoiled now and then. In 1970, Lee Parr McGrath and Joan Scobey published a collection of comments by children on grandmothers. It is called *What Is a Grandmother?* and it goes right to the heart of the matter. According to the children, grandmothers are people who play with you whether they are busy or not. They also cuddle children who have mumps. They are groovy, even if they are married to grandfathers. Reported a young man named Andy, "A grandma is made to spoil you and save you from your parents."

Who could ask for a more noble mission in life?

Without question, your time is the most precious gift you can give your grandchild. For the littlest grandchild, being rocked by Grandma is a special experience. The baby will respond to the strength and security found in Grandma's arms.

As the grandchildren grow, the things that grandmothers can share with them become more varied and more fun. Cookies and cakes taste twice as good as when they're made especially for the grandchild. A walk is a high adventure and not just a way to get from here to there. On the way to the supermarket with Grandma, the child can see butterflies and flowers. Perhaps he can watch a fire engine roar past, or he and Grandma can pause to watch a steamroller clanking along. Parents have busy schedules and heavy responsibilities. They may not have time for butterflies, fire engines and steamrollers, but grandmothers often do. They are, to quote the children, the people who play whether they are busy or not.

The cookies and the cakes and the expeditions to see fire engines and to explore woods and parks are delights to both grandparent and child. Even more delightful is the storytelling. Grandmother is the one who can tell the children about Mother or Dad. Grandma remembers what the parents were like when they were little and what they did. And, from a child's point of view, Grandmother is a person who has lived a long, long time—ages and ages—and who knows what it was like in the olden days.

Grandmother will be wise if she anchors the child in reality and makes sure he realizes that she never crossed the Great Plains in a covered wagon, churned her own butter or did her lessons by the light of a tallow candle. However, Grandma's stories of her own growing years can expand the child's awareness of the continuity of a family and all of life. When the child understands where Grandmother stands in relation to Mother and Daddy, he will better understand his own place in the family.

Grandmother's stories don't help only the grandchild. They help Grandma herself. They give her an opportunity to go back to her own childhood. She remembers the stories *her* grandmother told her and for her the world becomes a larger place. Because she has listened to her grandmother's tales, her memory can stretch back for several generations. Through her grandchild, her hopes go forward and she looks into the future when the child will be an adult and perhaps a parent himself.

In addition to sharing the family stories, you can participate in wonderful adventures in make-believe with your grandchild. You may want to reread some of the books that you loved as a child, or that you read to your own children. Or browse the bookstores for new stories. My grandchildren loved *The Little Engine That Could*. When they were a bit older I read *Charlotte's Web* to them. One of my all-time favorites is Margery Williams' *The Velveteen Rabbit*. This is a story about a stuffed toy who wants very much to be real and who learns from a shabby old toy horse how one goes about this. "Real isn't how you are made," says the horse. "When a child loves you for a long, long time, not just to play with you, but really loves you, then you become real . . ."

Children understand this because they have not yet become calculating or watchful or cunning. Reality is simple and open; it is loving and being loved, and Grandmother can be the beneficiary of this.

Does Grandma live on a very restricted budget?

The child will not care. Grandma is warm, cozy and loving, and she always has time. To the child, that is what is important.

Even if the grandmother doesn't live near the child—even if she makes her home in some distant part of the country—she can be warm, close and loving. She can set aside a special time for sharing with the grandchild.

If you are a grandmother at a distance and you take a trip, drop a postcard to your grandchild. Or send an occasional letter not to Mother or Daddy, but to young Johnny or Susie. Enclose a snapshot to show what you've been doing or where you've been going. Or send a picture of Mother or Daddy when they were small. It can be a keepsake which will find its way into the child's special collection of cherished possessions.

Of course there will be marvelous times when the grandchild comes to visit. Even if you can't splurge on expensive toys and fancy clothes, you can shop the garage sales for things that will appeal to the youngsters. And your own overstuffed dresser or closet may be crammed with the perfect things for dress-up—old jewelry, handbags, ties, shoes and hats which the grandchild will think are hilariously funny. Few grandchildren are ever bored with family photo albums or your collection of home movies!

Sometimes the grandmother is concerned not because she lives so far away, but because she lives so near the child. She can fear that the relationship with the grandchild will become humdrum and commonplace.

Today many grandparents actually live with their grandchildren so that the parents can work. This need not be a handicap to the grandmother who wants to establish a warm, special relationship with the grandchild. There is much to be said for the family that has three generations living under one roof. With love and understanding, life in such a family can be richer for the children, the parents and the grandparents.

Of course the role of grandmother is slightly different if she is a part of the household. She becomes a sort of secondary mother, and usually shares responsibilities with the parents, helping with the decision-making and the discipline.

If this is to be the arrangement, guidelines should be carefully established at the very beginning. There should be a clear understanding about feeding schedules, the type of food the child will have, who will take the responsibility for marketing, laundry, toilet training and other areas of child care. As the child grows older, he must learn what his responsibilities will be. The parents must always feel that the child will be cared for as they themselves would care for him, but they must understand, too, that Grandmother has beliefs and values. The relationships between the three generations will need to be reexamined at frequent intervals, and when problems come up, they should be aired immediately.

It is worth a great deal of effort to make an arrangement involving three generations successful. If child care is required and the grandparents are willing and able, it can be an excellent solution for working parents, and it can provide an ideal environment for the child.

Sometimes it is the grandparents who need care and not the grandchild. We all develop some infirmities as we age and the presence of a grandparent who isn't always jolly—or even comfortable—can give the child a chance to understand that age exists as well as youth. If children are to be complete people, they need to understand and care for older people. They need to see the entire spectrum of life.

Sometimes the generations need to be apart.

Grandmothers face the prospect of grandmothering with different degrees of dedication. I would be greatly amiss if I blithely assumed that all grandmothers enjoy caring for their grandchildren. Perhaps you do not, at least when the babies are very young. You should not feel guilty if this is the case. You may enjoy your grandchildren more when they are older.

The nice part about grandchildren is that you can enter their lives whenever you feel comfortable.

But you may not want to wait. You may be eager to be a grandmother, doing all the grandmotherly things. You may have perfected your recipe for cookies, knit several dozen booties and rehearsed all the favorite lullabies. You may then discover that the new family has decided to go it alone.

One grandmother I know said, "I did everything right. What did I do wrong?"

Probably she did nothing wrong. The young parents did not really mean to reject her; it is unfortunate that she felt hurt and disappointed. She should not have taken the decision personally.

Some young couples who plan to share the responsibilities of parenting and home management feel that, working together, they will be less dependent on others for assistance.

Some young couples are not comfortable taking help at first. They may be insecure in their new roles and they may need time before they can welcome a grandmother into their new lives. It is likely that after a while they will be more open about having grandmother as a part of their new family.

Grandmothers have to make sacrifices, but they can gain so many rewards. If you are reading this either before or immediately after your grandchild is born, it may seem that you will be giving a great deal. The first weeks of a child's life are difficult for the family. They are a time of adjustment, of working through complex new relationships. You may grow weary of showing sensitivity, understanding, discretion and kindness. "Is this really worth the trouble?" you may wonder. It is.

As the child grows, you will feel that you have helped create a solid foundation for the new family. You can look forward to a happy future with your child and your grandchild. You have started upon the wonderful, exhilarating career of being a grandmother. I like to think that grandmothers have a certain measure of invincibility. They get better with age, never worse. As the toy horse explained to the velveteen rabbit, "Generally by the time you are real most of your hair has been loved off, your eyes drop out and you get loose at the joints and very shabby. But these things don't matter at all, because once you are real you can't be ugly, except to people who don't understand."

Grandmothers are indeed real. And are they ever ugly? Surely not, for the children do understand.

Dear friend,

It has been great fun writing this book, and I am excited to think that as you read it, you will be starting on your new career as a grandmother.

My own personal experience as a grandmother has been very rewarding. Life is not always perfect, even for grandmothers, but it is an ongoing, three-generation growing experience. And there is no doubt that the very best part comes when you feel two soft little arms around your neck, and you hear the words,

"I love you, Grandma!"